Anxiety in Relationships

How to Break Free from Jealousy, Codependency, Attachment and Insecurities in Just 7 Steps

Rita Hayes

Table of Contents

Introduction

Anxiety does not empty tomorrow of its sorrows, but only empties today of its strength. –Charles Spurgeon.

Your partner should be your safe space. The idea of seeing them should fill you with excitement. So what do you do when you have a healthy relationship but the thought of your partner fills you with dread instead of joy? Do you find yourself overanalyzing every word that comes out of your partner's mouth? Do you panic at the first hint of a problem? You may be experiencing relationship anxiety. You are not alone. Thousands of people all around the world suffer from relationship anxiety. While it is common, that doesn't mean you and your relationship are doomed and I'm here to help ensure your relationship remains satisfying and successful.

Perhaps, you don't suffer from anxiety, but you can't seem to understand why your partner suddenly shuts down at the first signs of an argument. Do they snap at you when you aren't able to spend time with them? Are you still trying to figure out why seemingly small things upset them? While anxiety is an awful thing to experience first-hand, it isn't any easier if you're on the receiving end of someone else's anxiety. It can be confusing when you feel as if you're doing everything right, but you can't seem to keep your partner happy.

Anxiety In Relationships will become your new best friend, guiding you through every tumultuous step of your anxiety-ridden relationship. Today, people are too quick to walk away from a relationship as soon as it becomes a little tough, but relationships are hard work. Occasionally, your biggest obstacle will be your own mind. You can't outrun your brain and leaving your current partner because your anxiety constantly gets in the way only ensures you have the same issues with a different person in the future.

This book comes from a place of experience. There have been far too many times in my relationship where my first thought was to leave my partner because they simply dared to tell me I was doing something that they disagreed with. In retrospect, many of the concerns they brought up were valid but that didn't stop my brain from going into overdrive. "They hate me", "I'm a terrible person", and "They're going to dump me; I should leave them first." These are all thoughts that would go through my mind regularly. Do I still get them occasionally? Of course, but with plenty of hard work and practice, I can manage them in a way that I can fully enjoy my relationship. If my anxiety begins to act up, I can easily sit back and remind myself that my brain is lying to me and that my partner loves me.

My goal with *Anxiety In Relationships* is to help readers realize that just because you or your partner have relationship anxiety, it doesn't mean that the relationship is a lost cause. You can (and will) overcome your anxiety so that your relationships will be safe spaces. My story is the rule not the exception and this book will help you reach a peaceful space just like I have.

This book will teach you:

- how to cope with your anxiety
- how to deal with an anxious partner
- how to strengthen your relationship so anxiety can't deter it
- the best ways to manage your relationship anxiety.

However, before we can begin solving your relationship anxiety problems, we need to understand what relationship anxiety is and how to identify it. In Chapter one, we will cover everything you need to know about anxiety. Once you know what to be on the lookout for, you'll have a solid foundation to begin improving your relationship.

Chapter 1:

What Is Anxiety in

Relationships?

When you begin a new relationship, a little bit of anxiety is normal. You may be worried about whether the other person likes you or not or you're scared that you'll do something to embarrass yourself. Usually, these concerns fade as you get more comfortable with your partner and the anxiety you feel doesn't cause any issues. The problem comes in when the anxiety persists long into your relationship and it begins to cause problems for you and your partner.

If you're suffering from relationship anxiety, you may experience constant emotional distress or exhaustion, lack of motivation, or you might even begin to experience physical symptoms such as headaches. The torment that comes with relationship anxiety can be isolating but as unpleasant as these experiences are, they're common and manageable. Relationship anxiety can be caused by past relationships or childhood experiences or it could simply be hereditary.

While there is no formal diagnosis for relationship anxiety, it is easy to spot. In this chapter, we will look at what relationship anxiety is, what the signs are, and how relationship anxiety can impact the lives of the sufferer and their partner.

Signs Of Relationship Anxiety

As I've mentioned above, some anxiety in your relationship can be normal. If you start engaging in self-sabotaging behavior or you catch yourself doing a few of the things on this list, it's time to take a deeper look at yourself and start making some changes.

Doubting Your Partner's Feelings

Overthinking and anxiety go hand-in-hand. When you're experiencing relationship anxiety, small things will upset you. For example, your partner hasn't texted you back in four hours. Logically, you know that they have a busy day ahead of them and they probably haven't had time to check their phone. This doesn't stop you from imagining all the possible worst-case scenarios. You constantly tell yourself that your partner doesn't love you any more or they find you annoying and that's why they haven't responded. Everyone feels like this from time to time, but when these thoughts become prominent without any real reason, you have a problem.

When left uninterrupted, the feeling that your partner doesn't love you can quickly develop into the idea that they want to break up. This can lead to you wanting to leave your partner before they can leave. When you're constantly plagued with the fear that your partner is going to leave you, it can lead to you changing your behavior in order to make them stay.

Self Silencing

When your anxiety turns into a negative voice in your head that's constantly telling you that your partner is going to leave you, you might start doing whatever you can to ensure your partner stays. This is what we call self-silencing and it is when you don't speak up about things that bother you out of fear that you might upset your partner.

When you self-silence, you're preventing the problem from ever being solved. Communication is a massive part of a healthy relationship and when you avoid talking to your partner about things that bother you, you risk slowly starting to resent your partner. This behavior can seriously damage your relationship and while the idea of confronting your partner can be daunting, remember that disagreements are a normal part of any relationship. If you're able to tackle your disagreements as a team in a civil way, it will alleviate some of your anxiety if similar situations arise in the future.

Always Expecting the Worst

When your relationship is going well, it's safe to say that it's unlikely you and your partner will break up. For someone with relationship anxiety, this isn't the case.

You will constantly be expecting something negative to happen.

This can be detrimental to your relationship because when you're always waiting for a fight or a break up, you can't fully enjoy the good times you and your partner share.

Doubting Your Compatibility

This goes hand in hand with doubting your partner's feelings. Relationship anxiety can cause you to emphasize the smallest differences between your partner and yourself. Even when the relationship is going well, you tend to look for the tiniest differences in your personalities and use them as a way out.

You convince yourself that since you love eating out and your partner loves home-cooked meals, your relationship must be destined to fail. As much as you two have in common, you will never be exactly the same as another person. There is nothing wrong with that and you need to try to remind yourself that there is usually a way around the contrasting parts of your personalities.

Overthinking

If you find yourself freaking out because your partner forgot to say I love you before they hung up the phone, you could have an overthinking problem. Overthinking has always been something I struggle with daily and it just seeped over into my relationship when my partner and I started dating.

Overthinking is troublesome because it can quickly turn an insignificant thing that your partner said or done into a massive fight. By over-analyzing everything your partner does, all you're really doing is making yourself miserable. It's exhausting reading into everything to find a problem that never existed in the first place.

You need to remind yourself that not everything has a deeper meaning. Sometimes your partner is just forgetful or they might be dealing with their own demons. The best way to combat an overthinking brain is to speak to your partner. In my experience, if something my partner did was causing me anxiety, I would speak to them about it. Nine out of ten times I was simply overreacting and we were able to calm my anxiety with nothing more than a short conversation.

Making Comparisons

In a world where social media plays a large role in our everyday lives, comparing your life to others is easier than ever. It's also become more common, but when you find yourself constantly comparing your relationship to your friends' relationships or the ones you see on TV, you have a problem.

Every relationship is different. It's important to keep in mind that while a relationship might look perfect to you, there could be an endless amount of problems that the couple keeps a secret from the public eye.

Constant Need for Reassurance

Relationship anxiety is a breeding ground for insecurities. This can result in you needing your partner to remind you that they love you and that there's nothing to worry about all the time. Needing reassurance occasionally is perfectly fine, but when you expect your partner to constantly reassure you, it can get exhausting for them.

When your partner needs to tell you every day that everything is fine, it can make them feel as if they aren't a suitable partner, putting even more strain on your relationship.

Sabotaging The Relationship

If the anxiety you feel in your relationship is left untreated, you may begin sabotaging the relationship. Most people who suffer from relationship anxiety will look for ways out of their relationship before their partner can leave them first. Usually, you won't actively sabotage your relationship, but subconsciously, you will take part in activities that push your partner away.

This sabotage could look like picking fights with your partner for no reason, flirting with other people to see if your partner cares, or distancing yourself from them to see if they notice. You might do these things just to get some extra attention from your partner, but it's unlikely that they will see it that way.

When you start trying to sabotage your relationship, regardless of your reasons, you're only going to push your partner away. Instead of acting out, try to speak to your partner about your concerns so you can fix the issue together.

Attachment Styles

The attachment style theory was originally developed to explain the relationship between an infant and their parents but has more recently been used to describe the attachment styles of adults. (Ainsworth & Bowlby, 1991).

By understanding the four different attachment styles, you will gain a better insight into why certain people are more prone to relationship anxiety. It will also help you and your partner have a better understanding of each other. When you take each other's attachment style into consideration, it will only strengthen your relationship.

There are four main attachment styles which are broken up into two groups. The insecure attachment styles are anxious, avoidant, and disorganized attachment styles. There is only one secure attachment style of the same name. It's common to have a few traits from each style, but one style normally shines above the rest. To help you better understand the four attachment styles, I will give you a detailed look at each of them. While it may seem as though the anxious attachment style is the most likely to develop relationship anxiety, it is vital to understand all four.

Anxious Attachment Style

Also known as the preoccupied attachment style, the anxious attachment style is characterized by the fear of losing your partner. Someone with an anxious attachment style usually has low self-esteem while simultaneously putting their partner on a pedestal. The imbalance between their self-image and the image of their partner leads the person with the anxious attachment style to constantly seek out the approval of their partners. Their anxiety is easily calmed by a partner who gives them plenty of attention and support. However, when they don't receive that attention, an anxious attachment style is more likely to become clingy, difficult, and demanding.

An anxious attachment style can become draining for both parties in the relationship. It can cause unnecessary strain on the relationship, especially if your partner feels that they always need to be on their toes in case something they do upsets you. This attachment style stems from a fear of abandonment or trauma from past relationships or childhood. Finding out where this anxiety stems from is a great start to combatting this attachment style and maintaining a healthy relationship.

Avoidant Attachment Style

Unlike the anxious attachment style, people with an avoidant attachment style tend to have higher self-esteem. The lone wolves would typically be categorized in this attachment style. People with an avoidant attachment style are self-sufficient and independent and will avoid emotional closeness at all costs. They hold themselves in high regard and believe they don't need anyone else in their lives. They enjoy doing things on their own and despise depending on others or even having others depend on them. While it's not likely that this attachment style will be in a relationship when they are, it can be difficult for both parties. There will be an ongoing struggle because for the person with this attachment style, opening up and allowing their partner to see their vulnerable emotional side will always be a challenge. They will actively suppress their emotions and isolate themselves when they feel as though things are getting too serious.

Unlike the anxious attachment style, this isn't an attachment style you can work on as a couple. Finding the root of your avoidant attachment style is the only way to solve this problem. Of course, finding the root cause of your attachment style doesn't instantly solve the problem, but talking things out with your partner will help you manage your insecure attachment style.

Disorganized Attachment Style

Also known as the fearful-avoidant attachment style, the disorganized attachment style is more complicated than the other two insecure attachment styles. People with this attachment style are walking contradictions when it comes to relationships. While they crave the intimacy of a relationship, they still have a fear of being left by their partner. This can become frustrating for the partners of those with a disorganized attachment style. It might feel as though your partner is pulling away from you for no apparent reason whenever things start getting serious. It's important to note that this isn't always done intentionally.

While the main characteristics of the disorganized attachment style differ from the anxious attachment style, they both stem from some form of fear of abandonment. A partner with a disorganized attachment style may love you very much, but they're unable to suppress the anxiety they feel in their relationship. This is when they start pulling away and avoiding getting too emotionally close to their partners. As someone with a disorganized attachment style, you should prioritize finding the source of your abandonment fears. Another way to manage your disorganized attachment style is to be honest with your partner. Tell them when you're uncomfortable with how intimate you two are getting. This will help your partner understand when you become distant or they might be able to help you work through your attachment style issues. It always helps to have a fresh perspective on an old problem.

Secure Attachment Style

This is the only secure attachment style out of the four. It's also the healthiest attachment style to have. These are the people that are happy when they're single, but they're comfortable and secure when in a relationship. They don't need someone to improve their self-worth and to them, their relationships are just an added bonus. The key characteristics of a secure attachment style are high tolerance, craving emotional intimacy, actively turning to the support of their peers, and easily sharing their feelings with others.

Just because someone has a secure attachment style, it doesn't mean they're immune to insecure attachment characteristics. When you notice some insecure attachment style behaviors pop up, you should evaluate yourself and your relationships with others. When you do this regularly, it will drastically improve your approach to relationships.

Chapter 2:

How to Cope With Anxiety

in Relationships

I have an incredibly driven and hardworking partner. While this is a positive thing, it's also extremely difficult when you have relationship anxiety. There are days when I will only hear from them once or twice throughout the entire day. Those are the days I would question whether they still love me or not. I would convince myself that they're not responding to me because they find me annoying. I probably bothered him with my unending flow of messages asking if they still love me. I also have an understanding partner, but what do you do when your partner doesn't get why you need constant reassurance?

I have dated plenty of people who made me feel like I'm too much or I'm unlovable because I needed some extra reassurance every now and then. In retrospect, I wasn't an easy partner. I had a lot of work to do, but I can happily say I came out on top. In this chapter, we will take a look at ways to combat your relationship anxiety and the behaviors such as jealousy, codependency, and insecurities that come with it.

Relationship Anxiety and Jealousy

When relationship anxiety stems from low self-esteem, jealousy usually isn't far behind. We've all experienced jealousy at some point in our lives. When situations make you jealous, the jealousy passes just as suddenly as it appears, but sometimes jealousy sticks around. There's a reason why hundreds of books, movies, songs, and poems have been written about jealousy. For us to overcome our jealousy and to avoid things getting messy, we need to fully understand why we feel jealous and what our triggers are.

Jealousy in a relationship often comes from insecurities. Most of the time, these insecurities begin from an early age. Your parents or previous relationships play a big part in the way you act and feel in your present relationships. If you felt neglected by your parents as a child, you're likely to react in the same way you would have when you were younger in your present relationships. When we experience traumatic events, they fuel our inner critic. That little voice that never seems to stop telling you that you're not enough. This voice causes you to blame yourself for every tiny incident that happens whether it was your fault or not. This voice is responsible for thoughts that lead to jealousy such as "she's so much prettier than me." "He is much more successful than me." When you begin thinking these thoughts, you might subconsciously be pulling away from your partner in order to protect yourself.

How To Cope With Jealousy

Talk About It

Communication is essential in all relationships but when your inner critic is attacking yourself, speaking to your partner is easier said than done. This doesn't mean you should keep your feelings to yourself and allow them to take over your mind. Turning to a trusted friend or family member will help you make sense of your emotions. Speaking to someone else will help you put your emotions into perspective, especially if your jealousy is causing you to be irrational. Often we know when we're being irrational, but the critic inside our heads is much louder than our rational thoughts. This is why speaking to someone else is great. It's easier to listen to reason when it comes from someone you trust.

However, you can't keep putting off speaking to your partner forever. Seeking advice from those closest to you is a wonderful temporary fix but if your jealousy continues, the only way to address it is to speak to your partner. If you're unable to speak to your partner when things start bothering you, how will you ever trust them? A relationship without trust is a breeding ground for jealousy, creating an endless cycle of insecurity.

Confronting other people when they do something that upsets me has never been my strong point. To be frank, simply the thought of having to speak about my feelings filled me with anxiety. I always thought it was just better to remain silent. Everyone loves an easy partner, right? One that never argued, always smiled, and agreed to everything. Being pleasant never saved any of my past relationships. In fact, all it did was ensure that I was miserable while my partners continued to do everything I hated because they never knew any better. As I got older and learned more about myself, I understood that this isn't a sustainable way to maintain a relationship. In my current relationship, I make a conscious effort to always bring up any issues I have with my partner. I still find this terrifying, but it has only improved my relationship. When you openly communicate with your partner, it means that both of you can improve and work on the things that bother the other person. By doing this, you'll strengthen your relationship to a point where jealousy has no place in your relationship.

Pay Attention To Your Feelings

We know what jealousy feels like but what else happens inside when you begin to feel jealous? What was the cause of your jealousy? Does jealousy lead to anxiety or rage? Did something your partner do remind you of the way a previous partner treated you? By looking at every angle, you will start to identify patterns.

When you pay close attention to these patterns, you will be able to figure out what your triggers are and address them by yourself or with your partner. Most of the time your jealousy has little to do with your partner being untrustworthy and more to do with negative past experiences. By identifying and addressing them, you will be able to drastically minimize excessive amounts of jealousy.

Calm Down

When you're consumed with jealousy, the first thing you want to do is react. Whether that is by yelling at your partner or by pulling back and distancing yourself from them, it doesn't really matter. All that does matter is that when you react while emotional you're not going to solve anything; all you'll do is push your partner away. By doing this, you're setting up your relationship for even more jealousy. Keep in mind that just because your jealousy made you think something is happening doesn't make it true.

When you feel overwhelmed with anxiety, the best thing to do is stop and pause. We need to remind ourselves that having negative feelings such as jealousy is okay. You shouldn't negate yourself about it because that will only worsen your anxiety. When we learn to accept our emotions instead of fighting them, it becomes easier to deal with.

Later in this book, we will look into various tools you can use to fight your anxiety, but one of those tools that will help when jealousy pops up is to breathe. Taking slow, deep breaths is a perfect way to calm you down. It also allows you to really consider what your next course of action is instead of just reacting to your emotions without thinking. Once you've calmed down and cleared your head, you and your partner can tackle the situation while avoiding a fight.

No one is perfect. No matter how amazing and understanding your partner is, they're still human. You could think your partner is the best person on the planet for you but that doesn't mean they will never let you down. At the same time, nothing in life is guaranteed. This thought might be the reason for your jealousy, but the sooner you accept that fact, the easier it is to move forward. I could go on about ways to combat your relationship anxiety or your jealousy, but none of them will be successful if you don't work on your self-esteem. You don't have to instantly become the most confident person in the world, but it's crucial to learn how to love yourself without the love of others.

I have mentioned multiple times how jealousy and relationship anxiety stems from insecurity. When you're confident in yourself, you know that no matter what happens in your relationship you're going to be okay. Knowing this makes your relationship less scary. You'll be less concerned about other people interfering in your relationship and you'll be more focused on actually enjoying your relationship.

Relationship Anxiety and Codependency

A codependent relationship is characterized by one person's needs being met or prioritized more than the others. People with relationship anxiety are more likely to have codependency issues because of the constant need to keep their partner happy. In a codependent relationship, the anxious partner will feel more at ease when they're with their partner and they will do whatever they can to be around their partner as much as possible. When they're not around their partner, that's when the anxious feelings begin. They will start questioning their partner's loyalty and start overthinking every aspect of their relationship.

If you have codependent characteristics, you have a strong need for the approval of those around you including your partner, friends, family, or colleagues. The problem with co-dependent relationships is that you give little to no importance to your own needs. You're constantly concerned with the feelings of your partner and you avoid making your own decisions out of fear that it will make your partner unhappy. While caring about your partner's feelings, it is important in a relationship that you cannot put their feelings above your own because it will only make you miserable.

To a codependent person, being around their partner and enjoying life with them is their safe space. Normally when you have a positive time with your partner and they leave, you are left with a warm happy feeling. To a codependent person, this warm and happy feeling only exists when they are around their partner. As soon as their partner leaves, they are met with that familiar feeling of unease and that creates the need to be reassured by the partner all the time.

Another major concern of co-dependency is that a codependent person will try and fix everybody's problems and do everything for the partner instead of addressing issues as a team. This problem-solving mentality is used as a coping mechanism but left unmanaged, it can cause the person with co-dependency issues to burn out. Being a problem solver can also make that person feel more lonely. While they may be afraid to speak up regarding their own needs, they could still feel like their partner doesn't do enough to support them when they are in need.

How To Cope With Codependency

Know When to Take a Step Back

Helping and supporting your partner is important but you need to find the line between being helpful and being codependent. A person with core dependency issues will help their partners with ulterior motives such as keeping their partner in their relationship. They will see it as the more their partner needs them, the less likely they are to break up with them. Sometimes, the stars work and a co-dependent person's partner will start turning to them more often. As I mentioned earlier, this isn't a positive thing because you do run the risk of becoming exhausted because your needs aren't being met.

Set Boundaries

Having healthy boundaries in place will protect your energy and your mental health. Setting boundaries is not an easy thing to do. It's taken me years to learn how to do it successfully, but I'm here to help ensure that you're not stuck practicing this for years.

Setting boundaries doesn't mean that you can't be there to support your partner. When your partner comes to you with a problem, you can still sit and listen to them but unless they ask you for your advice or your help, just sit back and listen to them because that is probably all they need at the moment. Practicing just listening to your partner is a great and easy way to practice setting boundaries.

Another great method of boundary setting that you can practice before putting it into action is to learn how to say no. Just getting yourself accustomed to saying simple things like "I'm just not feeling up to that at the moment" is perfect to get you comfortable enough to actually say no when the situation requires it.

Lastly, when you've grown accustomed to being codependent on your partner, it is helpful to take a step back and question yourself before you act on the urges to just blindly help. Consider why we're helping whether you want to help if you have the capacity to help and if it will interfere with your own needs. This will help you evaluate the situation and figure out if you really need to act on your feelings.

Look For Patterns

Your past plays a massive role in how you act in your present relationships. Your attachment style especially is formed in your formative years and you will continue to repeat the same anxious cycles until you decide to work towards ending them.

By taking a step back when your anxiety and codependency start acting up, really pay attention to what caused the episode and notice similarities in your triggers. Once you have identified those triggers, you can go back to your past experiences and find the root cause of your codependency. When you combat your codependency at the source, you avoid any future fallouts with your partner because you've solved the main issue. The amount of smaller triggers will disappear.

Tips for Minimizing Relationship Anxiety

Work on Your Self Esteem

I have said many times in this book that having a high self-esteem is crucial for a healthy relationship. You don't wake up one day suddenly feeling confident so how do you boost your self-esteem?

Start writing down a few positive affirmations and read them out loud daily. This sounds ridiculous and you might feel awkward doing it at first but it works. When you hear something often enough, you will start to believe it. That being said, if you're anything like me and you use humor as a coping mechanism, you should stop making any self deprecating jokes. I know what you're thinking "they're so funny, they make me happy." This could be true, but it doesn't change the fact that when you keep saying negative things about yourself (even as a joke) you're going to start believing it. It's amazing what a difference changing the way you speak to yourself can make. At the beginning of my journey to manage my anxiety, I jokingly proclaimed that "I'm going to start acting super full of myself until I actually believe I am an incredible person." And it worked. I love the person I am.

Remember that it's okay to make mistakes. You're only human. A sure-fire way to send your self-esteem plummeting is to negate yourself every time you make an insignificant mistake. Instead of panicking over a mistake that has already happened, try to focus on what you can do. If you can reconcile the mistake, then you don't have to worry. If you can't reconcile the mistake, then wasting anymore time freaking out about it is counter productive. Go easy on yourself and find a way to distract you if you can't stop fixating on it.

Focus on the people and things that you love. An instant confidence booster is to surround yourself with things that bring you joy. It can be anything friends, a hobby, a favorite sweater, or your pets. When you're entertained and happy, all of your attention will be focused on whatever you're doing at that point. Your brain will be too busy to wander off into anxiety land.

Communication

Having uncertainty in your relationship is an easy way to bring anxiety into the mix. That's why communication is key to every successful relationship, but when you or your partner have relationship anxiety, communication can save your relationship.

By having an open line of communication between you and your partner, you will avoid any misunderstandings. An anxious partner will overanalyze everything so when the two of you address any issues as soon as they come up and you set clear expectations for each other, there will be little room for overthinking.

Setting clear expectations for you, your partner, and your relationship early on will ease some of the stress that may come up later. When both of you know what to expect from the relationship, it is less likely that either of you will develop relationship anxiety.

Just make sure that when you need to have a serious conversation, you do it face to face. Texting is great when you need to address a serious situation and you have anxiety, but it can be tricky. For example, it's impossible to pick up on tone through a text message which can often lead to fights when one person isn't understanding the message properly.

Always be respectful of your partner. Disagreements happen even in the best relationships but even when you don't agree with your partner, you should always be kind to them. You will come to an agreement eventually or you'll agree to disagree and move on, but moving on is significantly more difficult if you were cruel to your partner. If you're not the best at keeping your cool during important discussions, writing down everything you want to say will help. When you've written down your feelings before the discussion, you would have had time to get your feelings out and compose yourself so you have a clear and level head when speaking to your partner.

Stay True To Yourself

As your relationship grows, you and your partner will grow with it. Small changes to your personality during a relationship is expected. You will start picking up some of their traits and they will pick up some of yours. If you find yourself starting to drastically change your personality to please your partner, it can lead to insecurities because it removes any sense of self that you had.

Your partner was attracted to you for a reason so there is no need to change your personality to please them. You could cause strain on your relationship if you've become a completely new person and they've stayed the same.

Chapter 3:

How to Cope With a

Partner Who Has Anxiety

If you've never experienced anxiety, the actions of an anxious partner won't make much sense to you. As much as you love your partner, it's hard to be understanding when to you it seems as though they're being irrational. In this chapter, I will go over a few situations that cause anxiety and ways to help you keep your partner feeling safe and free from anxiety. This chapter will also help to give you a sense of security in the relationship. By having a better grasp on what is going on in your partner's head, you can tackle the relationship anxiety as a team.

Causes Of Relationship Anxiety

Everyone is different and their triggers will be different but there are a few common causes for relationship anxiety.

Money

Money stresses all of us out in normal circumstances and that stress only gets more intense when you throw a relationship into the mix. Many people tend to hide parts of their financial situations away from their partners until something major happens. Shame over losing a job or spending money can cause you to feel insecure about yourself and where you stand with your partner.

Even if you and your partner are 100% honest with each other regarding your financial standings, money can still be stressful. For example, if you're doing well with money but your partner is a starving artist, that can be endearing until you live together and need to pay bills. If you're the only one covering living expenses, it can be stressful and it could turn a once endearing trait into something that you resent. While you're frustrated, your partner might be overcome with anxiety.

Unless you suddenly win the lottery, there's no easy way around money stress. Your best course of action would be to avoid keeping secrets from each other and be open about everything from the get-go.

Love

We all have a small amount of anxiety when you're starting a new relationship but once you have fallen deeply in love, that anxiety should subside if not completely disappear. Falling in love might make you realize that now you need to start sharing more personal information with your partner. If you have a partner with an avoidant or disorganized attachment style, the thought of opening up emotionally can be terrifying.

When you've had toxic relationships in the past, falling in love will seem more like a nightmare than a dream. An anxious partner could look at your new found love as having more to lose.

Fear

There are two main fears that drive relationship anxiety: the fear of losing your partner and the fear of being abandoned. The problem with fear is that it consumes every part of your being. If your partner is being driven by fear, they will find it impossible to enjoy the good times the two of you have because they're so focused on ways to make sure you don't leave.

You might not suffer from relationship anxiety, but all of us have experienced fear. You know it can make you do unusual actions. Reminding yourself that your partner is likely acting out of fear is a start to understanding why they act the way they do.

How to Calm Your Partner Down

For the most part, anxiety needs to be dealt with by the person who is suffering from it but that doesn't mean you're helpless. No one wants to see a loved one suffer so below I've written down a list of a couple of simple things you can do to help your partner feel more at ease in your relationship.

Address Their Symptoms

Most of the solutions I can give you regarding relationship anxiety involve positive communication. If your partner begins showing signs of relationship anxiety, the best place to start is to sit down and figure out which of their actions was done in response to anxiety. This is going to help you figure out what direction the two of you need to go in to soothe their anxiety. Having an open discussion about your partner's symptoms will also help you figure out when something is negative about your relationship or if it's just their anxiety.

When you begin this discussion, ask your partner "What causes you stress?" or "What are your main stressors?" When you don't call the anxiety anxiety, it makes it less intimidating so the two of you can have an easier time addressing your partner's anxiety.

Don't Minimize Their Feelings

Anxiety can be scary for those suffering from it. The last thing your partner needs is their favorite person making them feel negative about their anxiety. Their actions might not make sense to you, but to them, it will seem like they're making the most logical decisions.

People with anxiety require plenty of validation. If you tell them that you think they're being ridiculous, they're not going to listen to logic. All you'll be doing is making them feel more insecure which will make the situation worse.

Instead, make your relationship a judgment free zone. When your partner comes to you about their anxiety, focus on being compassionate first. Once you can see that they've calmed down, then you can start focusing on a logical approach.

Don't Be Forceful

Having an anxious partner can be frustrating for you, but they're probably just as frustrated as you are. Your brain being in overdrive and constantly looking for the worst case scenario is exhausting. Be kind to your partner.

Try to control your frustration and encourage your partner instead of attacking them. If their anxiety is especially negative, they're going to have a negative outlook on every aspect of their lives. Your job is to focus on the positives especially if their anxiety is stopping them from doing something. Let your partner know that you understand why they're feeling anxious and that their feelings are valid. Once you've reassured them, you can start encouraging them. Instead of questioning them about why they won't do something, tell them why it's a great idea to do it.

Management Not Banishment

Anxiety is your body's natural response to danger. When humans still lived in the wild, we needed our anxiety to know it's time for fight or flight. Today, we don't have to worry about being eaten by lions, but we have many other stressors in our lives and our minds trick our bodies into thinking you're actually in danger. This is when anxiety becomes a problem. It's taken centuries of evolution for our bodies to develop this skill so your partner's anxiety isn't going to go away overnight. The goal is to help them manage their anxiety, not get rid of it.

Successfully managing anxiety means that even if some situations make them anxious, they're not crippled by the anxiety. For example, if you're afraid of boats, you might have a full blown panic attack before boarding so you decide to stay on land. Having a grip on your anxiety means that even though you still have a fear of boats, you're able to compose yourself enough to get on the boat and even enjoy it.

Live Your Life

It's natural to want to help your partner as much as possible but just because you don't have relationship anxiety or an insecure attachment style doesn't mean that your feelings aren't important. If you neglect your mental health so you can focus on your partner's, you could end up being the partner with relationship anxiety. If your relationship is being overshadowed by anxiety, you need to find an occasional escape. I don't mean to say you should leave your partner hanging but it's impossible to pour from an empty cup. You need to make sure you're happy before focusing on anyone else, no matter how much you love them.

You shouldn't allow your partner's anxiety to consume your life. Be sure to set your own boundaries. Let your partner know if you're not doing very well mentally and you just don't have the capacity to help with their anxiety. Finally, find some time to do the things you love including sports, video games, fitness, or even having a drink with a friend.

Chapter 4:

Tips to Minimize Anxiety

Those who have been diagnosed with an anxiety disorder are more likely to develop relationship anxiety. Combatting your regular anxiety before it can turn into relationship anxiety will make navigating your relationship a breeze.

Mindfulness

Mindfulness is a way to train yourself to be completely present in every thing you do. All of your attention is focused on the task at hand. As someone with anxiety, mindfulness has always been a struggle but when you get the hang of it, it's close to magic. The anxious mind is a restless mind. Your brain goes a hundred miles an hour, replaying the embarrassing things you've done in the past or dreading the future.

By practicing mindfulness, you're training your brain to stop wondering and enjoy the moment. Have you ever done a task that required your full attention? When you read a book or you're doing an important project for work you don't have the time to think about anything else. Next time you're engulfed in an activity, think about how you feel. Do you feel anxious at all? The chances are your answer is going to be no because it's hard to feel anxious when all of your brain capacity is going to whatever you're doing. Mindfulness gives you that peaceful feeling but removes the distraction. For people who meditated for 8 weeks, a significant change in the participants' blood pressure as well as a significant change in 172 genes in regulating inflammation, circadian rhythms and glucose metabolism occurred (Bhasin et al., 2018).

How Do I Practise Mindfulness?

Mindfulness isn't only about being present. It's about being present without judgement. Our entire lives are spent building up our ego through our life experiences. Your ego is the one that causes you to harshly judge others and yourself. If your inner critic's voice is loud, chances are that it'll be a challenge to silence your ego. To improve your mindfulness skills, you need to meditate. When you think of meditation, you probably picture a monk sitting on the ground with his legs crossed and his eyes closed. This is a form of meditation, but if you've got the voices of your inner critic and your judgmental ego floating about in your head, just sitting quietly will quickly become a nightmare. When I tried to meditate like I've seen countless times in movies and TV shows, it seemed as though my brain actually sped up instead of slowing down. You're always told to focus on your breath, but when you're trying to calm your anxiety, focusing on breathing could make it worse. Luckily for us, all hope isn't lost because there are plenty of different ways to meditate. You just need to find the method that works best for you.

Guided Meditation

If you're unsure of how to properly meditate, guided meditation is the way to go. Guide meditation is a meditation led by an instructor. Even if you know how to meditate but you struggle to stay focused on your own, guided meditation is the one for you.

In a guided meditation, your instructor will either give you instructions that you need to follow or they will create a scene that you can immerse yourself in. Aside from the fact you will have an expert with you through your entire meditation journey, concentrating on your teacher's voice prevents your thoughts from straying.

There are many ways to participate in guided meditations. You can take a look online for meditation classes in your area if you'd like a face to face experience. We're using meditation to combat anxiety and I know anxiety can make leaving your house feel like you're going to way so you might not want to go out and have to interact with a stranger. If this is the case for you, you don't have to give up on guided meditation before you start. There are plenty of meditation apps and YouTube videos that you can play for free in the comfort of your own home.

Focused Meditation

When practicing focused meditation, you use one or more of your senses. Just like the name suggests, this form of meditation requires a large amount of concentration. Many beginners struggle with this method for that very reason. However, if you feel this is the best meditation method for you and you happen to lose your focus, don't worry, take a deep breath and start again. With practice, you will be able to hold your focus for longer and longer.

In order to do focused meditation, you will need something that you can keep your attention on. This can include counting your breaths, looking into a candle flame, looking at nature, or listening to specific sounds such as Tibeten singing bowls.

Mantra Meditation

Have you ever watched a movie about Buddhist monks and when they show a scene where they're meditating, you always hear one sound "ohm, ohm, ohm." What you were watching was mantra meditation. You're not limited to using ohm if you choose to do a mantra meditation.

You can choose any word or phrase that resonates with you and you repeat that out loud until your meditation is over. Having a single word or sentence to focus on makes staying present during your meditation much easier. You can even kill two birds with one stone by making your mantra something positive and uplifting about yourself. By repeating a positive message over and over, it will eventually be solidified in your mind, improving your mindfulness and your self-esteem all at once.

Progressive Relaxation

Better known as movement meditation, progressive relaxation is the act tensing and relaxing your muscles in order to relieve tension in the body. Progressive relaxation is awesome because you don't need any instructor or videos to do it.

All you need to do is lay on your back and close your eyes. With your eyes still closed, slowly tense up your feet muscles and hold it for a few seconds and then release. After your feet, move on to your legs muscles and do the same. Repeat this process with the muscles in your entire body all the way up to your face.

We hold so much tension in our bodies that we don't even realize, by doing this meditation you can release that tension, leaving you feeling light and free.

Visualization Meditation

In visualization meditation, you're taking what you've learned during your guided meditation practices and doing them on your own. In this form of meditation, you picture positive scenes or images in hopes of creating a more tranquil inner environment.

Think of the visualization meditation as a daydream with a purpose. You focus your energy on creating a detailed scene that brings you joy. There are no rules to what you can visualize and it should make you feel happy. You could imagine yourself finally succeeding at a goal like getting the promotion you've been working for or you could create a scenario where you get to spend time with a loved one who passed away. No matter what you decide to imagine during your visualization meditation you're guaranteed lower stress levels, a better overall mood, and a feeling of peace within.

Yoga

Yoga technically is considered a movement meditation but movement meditation isn't limited to yoga. It can be any form of soft movements from tai chi to walking. Before I knew anything about mindfulness and treating my anxiety, I started yoga as a new way to stay fit. It took me less than a week to notice that once I finished my yoga routine, I was filled with more peace than I had ever been in. As someone who's obsessed with researching everything, I immediately went to look up why I felt so great after a yoga session.

If you've ever done yoga before, you'll know that they put a lot of importance on your breathing and every movement is intentional. Since you're so focused on maintaining a steady breath while holding all of the complex positions, you clear your mind of any other thoughts. Since I first started doing yoga, it's changed from a way to stay fit to a vacation for my mind. I hate exercising and I regularly have days where I get on my yoga mat and count every torturous second until the workout is over, but sometimes it's different. Regularly when my mental health goes downhill, I find myself craving a yoga workout, even if it's been months since my last one.

One thing I hate more than working out is working out in public which is one of the few things my anxiety still won't allow. Most gyms hold yoga sessions weekly and sometimes daily and if that's your thing, then go and do a group yoga session for the both of us! If you're like me and you feel like you're going to embarrass yourself in front of a class, there are lots of videos online that you can stream for free just like with guided meditation. I love the fact that I can pretty much have an instructor-led class without the added anxiety of learning a new skill in front of a room full of people.

Stay Healthy

When you suffer from anxiety, your head is full of thoughts all the time. Maintaining a healthy lifestyle will keep your head clear and improve your concentration. It's also a common fact that when you look better, you feel better.

Eat regular healthy meals and never skip any of them, especially breakfast. Breakfast kicks starts your metabolism and gets rid of that groggy feeling we all get in the morning.

Another key part of staying healthy is to exercise regularly. I have already gone over the benefits of doing yoga but any workout will leave you feeling energized, refreshed, and calm. When you exercise, your body releases hormones called endorphins, also known as the feel good hormone. Endorphins drastically improve your mood; there's a reason many runners refer to a "runners high" that they get after a successful run.

As a result of keeping up with a healthy lifestyle, you'll start looking more toned. When you start noticing the results of your clean living, your confidence will instantly shoot up.

Breathe

Poor breathing can cause anxiety and panic attacks. During a panic attack when your body thinks it's in danger, it will limit the oxygen flow through your body, resulting in shallow breaths. Those short breaths kick start your body's fight or flight process, worsening your anxiety. When this happens, your anxiety might cause physical symptoms such as body tremors, muscle tension, dizziness, and an increased heart rate. By taking long, controlled breaths you counteract these sensations. Breathing techniques will also calm you down instantly, but it can also be used to prevent anxiety all together.

Just like meditation, there is more than one way to practise improving your breathing.

4-7-8 Breathing

The 4-7-8 breathing method is also known as the relaxing breath. This technique is considered a natural sedative, making it an ideal exercise for the anxious mind. When you do this technique, it's best to sit up straight at first, but once you've gotten the hang of it, you can even lay down in bed and do this.

To do this technique, start by placing your tongue on the roof of your mouth. Next, you need to take a loud, deep breath. Make a whooshing sound when you're doing this. You might feel a bit silly making that much noise but stick to it and soon you won't think twice about it.

After your exhale, close your mouth and take a long, slow breath in and count to four. Hold that breath in for seven seconds and then do your loud exhale once again for eight seconds.

Repeat this exercise as many times as you feel necessary.

Box Breathing

Also known as four square breathing, box breathing focuses on keeping your breaths in a steady rhythm. I was taught this method years ago by my therapist and I love it because it's so easy and you can do it anywhere.

Breathe in for four seconds. You can do any type of exhale for this exercise so if you're in a public space, you can just do quiet breaths. Hold your breath in for four seconds and then exhale for another four seconds. Hold your breath for four seconds and then repeat.

Alternate Nostril Breathing

Alternate nostril breathing involves blocking one nostril while breathing through the other in a set rhythm. Doing this exercise helps you pay closer attention to your breathing, improving your mindfulness while calming yourself down. It's best to do this technique while sitting.

To start, bend the pointer and middle finger of your right hand and hold your right nostril closed. Leave your pinky finger, ring finger, and thumbs extended. This is actually a yoga pose called Vishnu Mudra.

Once you've securely closed your right nostril, close your eyes or hold a soft gaze and inhale through your left nostril. How long you choose to inhale and exhale is up to you, but an amount of time would be three seconds.

After your inhale keep the same hand position but switch to your left nostril and exhale through your right nostril.

Take another inhale through your right nostril; then switch so you can exhale through your left nostril.

Try to repeat this cycle ten times. If you start to feel light headed, it's okay to pause so you can breathe through both nostrils at once.

Belly Breathing

Practicing belly breathing for about 20 minutes every day will drastically lessen your anxiety. 20 minutes is a long time and when you're starting out, you might not be able to hold your focus for that long. Starting small is okay; no one is a professional at first. Instead of trying to go for the full 20 minute exercise, start off by doing three breath cycles and then gradually increase how long you practice.

Belly breathing is great because you can prioritize comfort; all you need is somewhere that's quiet. Whether you choose to sit on your couch, lay on your bed, or sit on the floor with your legs crossed, it will work perfectly. The only requirement is that you put one hand on your chest and one on your stomach just below your ribs.

Now that you've got your position down, you're ready to start your practice. Start by relaxing your stomach, don't suck it in or clench it and take a deep breath in through your nose. The hand that's on your belly should move up and down with each breath.

Next, slowly exhale through your nose. When you exhale, pay close attention to the hand on your chest. It shouldn't be moving at all when you breathe.

By shifting your attention to your hands, you minimize the chances of your mind wandering off.

Simple breathing

Simple breathing can be done as many times as you need. This technique is great if you're anxious and you can feel a panic attack beginning. You can do simple breathing in any position, no matter where you are.

As the name states, this technique is simple, but it's not as easy as it may seem. With this technique, you don't have anything like your hands or counting to focus on so it's easier for your mind to wander off. There have been many times when I was feeling anxious and I wanted to try a breathing technique, but I couldn't silence my brain. This would often leave me feeling frustrated and defeated. If this happens to you, it's best to just stop trying because it will only make you feel worse. Instead try to practice another time when you're feeling less anxious, that way it's less frustrating for you. If you practice your breathing before you actually need it, it will be more effective when you need to soothe your anxiety.

To start, relax your entire body. Be mindful of the muscles in your face, jaw, and shoulders because we tend to hold all of our tension there without realizing it. Have you ever been told not to clench your jaw and suddenly you realized that you could take someone's arm off with how tightly you were holding it? Whenever I get told to relax my muscles, I'm always surprised to find how tense I actually was.

Once you're ensured that your body is relaxed, take a slow breath in through your nose. Just like belly breathing, your stomach should rise and fall with each breath but your chest should have little movement.

Exhale through your mouth but instead of just letting the breath flow out, try to blow. If it helps imagine you're blowing out a candle. You should hear a soft whoosh when you do this.

Repeat this exercise until you've calmed down.

Accept Being Out of Control

Wanting to be in control of every aspect of our lives is part of being human. However, life is unpredictable and it doesn't always go according to our plans. When you have your life in control, you feel safe and we all strive to feel safe and secure as often as possible. When you feel as if your life is spiraling out of control, you start to feel anxious. This lack of control is even more prominent in a relationship because now, you have to consider someone else. People are more unpredictable than life. They have their own complex emotions and you won't be able to dictate every aspect of your partner's life. Letting go of control means letting go of anxiety.

When you're not in control, you're filled with uncertainty and fear. Fear is a breeding ground for anxiety. Something that I've found helps me when I feel as though things aren't going my way is to remind myself that the negative thing has already happened and I can't change it so there's no reason for me to freak out about it. Instead I focus on ways to improve the situation.

Lack of control means you're likely to be less satisfied with life. Even if everything is going perfectly for you, you might still be focusing on the fact that the situation didn't go according to your plan. This can lead to you being your worst critic. You'll start fixating on every thing that's going negatively and out of your control. If you keep following this cycle, you're only going to make yourself miserable.

Nonviolent communication may also help with accepting things as they are in your relationship (Rosenberg, 2015). This method discusses how another person's actions are not personal. It's important to see this as someone's actions would likely have occurred in a situation with someone else. By understanding that, your own anxious feelings will likely dissipate when issues arise in the relationship.

When you learn to accept the things you can't change, you're opening up your life to more peace.

Distract Yourself

Distracting yourself isn't a long term fix, but it definitely helps when your anxiety is high. There is a fine line between helpful and hurtful when it comes to distraction. If your only way to calm your anxiety is to distract yourself, your distractions might turn into maladaptive behaviors. Maladaptive behaviors will make you feel better temporarily but in the long run, it will make your anxiety worse. Instead you should start practicing distraction techniques as a healthier way of keeping your mind occupied. Healthy distractions help you take your mind off of your negative emotions and allow you to focus your energy on a more positive activity. In the long term, using distraction techniques will help you regulate your emotions better.

Drink More Tea

This might seem like a strange solution to your anxiety, but many teas have calming properties. If you're stumped about what to do with your anxiety, taking the time to pause and make yourself a cup of tea will soothe your anxious state of mind. The most common calming tea is chamomile, but there are plenty of other teas you can drink if chamomile isn't for you.

Mint Tea

Mint tea is full of calming properties and it tastes delicious. Some types of mint tea may contain caffeine which is known to worsen anxiety. If the caffeine levels in mint tea concern you, an alternative is peppermint tea. Peppermint tea will relax you just as well as mint tea but without the caffeine.

Chamomile

As I mentioned above, chamomile is the most well known tea to combat anxiety. It's also packed with antioxidants so you can improve your health a bit while decreasing your anxiety.

Matcha

Matcha's popularity has increased over the last few years. There is a reason that matcha is so popular and it's not only because it tastes amazing. Matcha contains a higher dose of an amino acid called L-theanine than other teas. L-theanine plays a major role in relieving stress and anxiety.

The combination of L-theanine and caffeine works to put your body into a meditative state that matcha lovers refer to as a body high.

Lavender Tea

Using lavender to combat your anxiety isn't a new thing. There are plenty of lotions and body washes that include lavender. Many of them stating on the bottles that it will calm you down. But did you know that lavender can actually be made into a tea? Drinking lavender tea regularly will boost your feelings of relaxation more than any lotion or body wash would.

Rose Tea

Roses have been used for centuries for many reasons. When you drink rose tea, it gives you a mild euphoric feeling that will instantly put a stop to any anxiety you have.

Please note that I am not a medical professional and you should ask your doctor about the above natural remedies as some people may have allergies to certain foods and herbs.

Therapy

Unfortunately, there is still a stigma attached to mental health and going to therapy. This can make the idea of going to therapy scary for many people, but the benefits of going to therapy appropriate for you can help depending on what works for you.

Using different coping strategies will help you manage your anxiety but what happens when your anxiety keeps returning? A therapist will help to teach you new ways to manage your anxiety.

A common form of therapy used to treat anxiety is cognitive-behavioral therapy (CBT). With CBT, your therapist will help you get to the bottom of your anxiety. They will also help you to identify what your anxiety triggers are so that you can work together to get rid of it. When I first started therapy, I couldn't figure out why I was feeling anxious. All I knew was that I had anxiety. After a few sessions, it became apparent that a lot of my anxiety stems from my experiences with my family in my childhood. Once I knew where my anxiety came from, my therapist and I could begin rewiring my brain so that it no longer made the connections between my past and present experiences. Art therapy, nature based therapy, and other forms of therapy can also be effective for anxiety conditions.

We're all different. That's why going to therapy is so helpful. I can go on and on about how to combat your anxiety, but they might not work for you. By going to therapy, you will receive a personalized plan to get rid of your anxiety without having to try every single coping strategy.

Medication

If none of your other coping mechanisms are working, you might be prescribed anti-anxiety medication. The main form of anti-anxiety medication is benzodiazepines. This should be used as a last resort because most anti-anxiety medications are highly addictive.

Although they are addictive, there are also plenty of benefits to taking them. When you're on the verge of a panic attack, taking some medication can help before the pill takes effect. Once you take that pill, you know that help is on the way and anxiety will be gone soon and that thought alone can calm you down significantly. I would recommend seeking a medical professional's advice about taking anti-anxiety medications if you feel that you need to do so.

Chapter 5:

Strengthening Your

Relationship

We loved with a love that was more than love. –Edgar Allan Poe

When there is uncertainty in your relationship, that's when relationship anxiety pops up. By working together with your partner to strengthen your relationship, you lower the risk of developing anxiety. When you know that your relationship is solid, you'll be less scared if a disagreement comes up. You'll be sure that you and your partner will get through whatever problem you may be facing.

It doesn't matter if you and your partner have been dating for three months or three years, you still need to work to keep the romance alive once the honeymoon phase has ended. Life can become hectic sometimes and that could affect how you treat your partner which is why you need to work to keep your relationship healthy.

In this chapter, we will focus on how to improve the connection between you and your partner.

Quality Time

Our idea of how much time is enough time together will vary. You might feel like seeing each other once a week is enough but your partner might expect to see you more often than this. The two of you should schedule a time to discuss what you expect of each other in terms of quality time. If your expectations are very different, this will help you reach a compromise so that you both feel satisfied.

When I say you should spend quality time together, I don't mean just laying in bed mindlessly scrolling through your phones. You should make the most of the time you have with your loved one, especially if that time is limited.

If you're not able to see each other in person due to other commitments, you can still spend some time together. My partner and I have unusual schedules and we can't always visit each other so instead we'll stream a movie online together. When we do this, we will stay on the phone with each other so that we can discuss the movie while we watch. There are plenty of apps you can download that will sync up your videos so that it feels like you're actually together.

When the two of you do see each other, try to plan some fun activities so that your time together is memorable. In my experience, every time my partner and I decide to spend a full day together and we go on a bunch of adventures I always feel elated when I go home. You can find me roaming around the house with the biggest smile on my face for a few days after.

Try something new together like taking a cooking class. You will both always remember that activity as something exclusive to the two of you. If you take a cooking class and you make the dish you were taught when you're on your own, it will bring up a fond memory of your partner. You can even pick a book to read together and schedule regular check-ins where you can talk about what you've read together.

You don't always have to spend money to have a meaningful time together. Go on a hike together or if you don't have hiking spots where you live, a simple walk around a park or your neighborhood will do wonders too.

Listen

We know that having positive communication is important, but that's impossible if you're not listening to each other. When you feel like your partner genuinely cares about what you're saying when you're speaking about the unimportant things, you'll feel more comfortable when it comes to talking to them about your feelings.

Many of us think that we're great listeners but will fail to recount the last conversation we had with our partners. We listen to respond instead of fully taking in what our partner's say. If you do this in an argument, you could make your partner feel invalid and cause even more frustration. That's why it's vital to practice active listening when speaking to your partner. Just like meditation, active listening takes practice. By truly listening to your partner, it will encourage them to continue speaking to you openly about problems that arise in the relationship. When you actively listen to what your partner is saying, it shows that you don't allow your emotions to get the better of you, especially in a fight. It will also make your partner feel happy when they see that you're engaged in what they're saying.

You can show your partner that you're listening to them by asking questions and making an effort to really understand what they're saying. Once they have said what they need, you can give them a short summary of what they were speaking about. This will show them that you were paying attention but it will also ensure that you understood what they were saying correctly. If by chance you misinterpreted something they said, this will be the time that they can clarify the situation and put you at ease.

Build A Friendship

Relationships aren't all about romance. Most of us choose our partners based on physical attraction, but for a relationship to last there needs to be more than attraction. If you prioritize building a friendship with your partner, you will start enjoying your relationship a lot more. Your partner should be your best friend and when you treat them accordingly, you will make them feel loved and appreciated.

You can build your friendship by doing the same things you do to improve your relationship. You should work on really getting to know your partner. Play a game of 21 questions. It might seem like a strange thing to do if you and your partner have been dating for a while but it works. As we grow our likes and interests will change too so playing games that help you get to know each other is a fun way to form a deeper connection with your partner.

Date Nights

Building a friendship is important but so is being romantic sometimes. If you and your partner lead busy lives or money is tight, going out for a fancy dinner every weekend might not work. Set aside a date once a month where you two can get dressed up and go to dinner.

Date nights are great because you two get to do something outside of your regular routine and you'll have some uninterrupted quality time. When it's just the two of you sitting at a table, it's the perfect time to really talk to your partner. You can use this time to tick off a few other relationship strengthening activities like building your friendship, listening, or showing affection. You can also use this time to check in on each other and address any issues you may have at the time.

Learn Your Partner's Love Language

No one expresses love in the same way but how we love can be broken down into five love languages (Chapman, 1992). Those love languages are physical touch, quality time, acts of service, gift giving, and words of affirmation. Knowing what your partner's love language is will give you some insight into how you should show them affection and visa versa.

By knowing what your partner's love language is you will become more thoughtful with how you treat them.

Below I will go into detail of each love language but if you're still unsure of what your love language is, you can find a love language quiz with a quick Google search.

Physical Touch

People who have physical touch as their loved language will feel their happiest and most loved when their partner shows them signs of affection such as kissing, holding hands, sex, and cuddling.

If your partner's love language is physical touch, they will feel more connected to you when you show them affection in this way. You'll also make them feel more appreciated and they will likely do the same for you, further enriching your relationship.

Quality Time

When your love language is quality time, you'll feel the best when your partner makes an active effort to spend time with you. People whose love language is quality time will love it when you show them that they have your undivided attention.

If you take this type of love language into consideration and you act on it to make your partner feel loved, you will be improving your relationship at the time. This is because quality time is important even if neither of you have it as a love language. This way you're killing two birds with one stone.

Acts Of Service

Those whose love language is acts of service love it when their partner does things to make their life easier. These acts of service don't need to be big. It can be the small things like making them a coffee in the morning or washing their dishes when they're not feeling up to it.

People with this love language take the saying "actions speak louder than words" seriously. They don't want you to tell them how much you love them. They want you to show them.

Gift Giving

Similar to the acts of service love language, people whose love language is gift giving prefer to be shown that they're loved rather than being told. They're not too concerned with how much money you spend on their gifts, rather they appreciate that you took the time to choose something meaningful to give them. When you bring them gifts without the need of a birthday or special occasion, it shows that you're thinking of them when you're not together. This makes them feel appreciated and loved.

Words Of Affirmation

If your love language is words of affirmation, you won't be too bothered by fancy gifts or other displays of affection. People with this love language needs you to tell them outright how much you love them. While they adore being told "I love you", there are many other ways to express your love. This includes giving them compliments regularly, encouraging them, and texting them frequently.

Being told that they're loved and special will make them content in the relationship because they always feel appreciated.

Show Affection

Everyone wants to be reminded that they're loved. Doing small things to show your partner you love them will help make them feel more secure in your relationship. You know that you love your partner but if you don't express it, how will they know? Showing affection can be anything from grabbing their hand when you're walking in the grocery store.

When it comes to showing affection, you should be mindful of falling into a routine. An affection routine is when you only express your love out of habit. Maybe you only tell them you love them just before you go to bed but never any other times or you only give them a quick kiss in the mornings. While doing these things isn't negative, in fact, they are positive things to do. It can quickly become monotonous and your partner will pick up on that. Instead show your affection when your partner least expects it. This will show them that you're thinking about them and it will make them feel more loved.

Focus On the Small Things

Has someone ever told you something about yourself that you mentioned in passing months ago? If this has happened to you, you know how special it makes you feel. When you really listen to what your partner says and you remember tidbits about them, you show them that you truly care about what they have to say.

Paying more attention to them will help you navigate the relationship with more ease too. They might mention something that they really want and if you remember, you can buy it for their birthday. If they mention a new food place, they want you to take them on a date to that place.

The small things add up eventually and when you keep doing them, your relationship overall will improve and grow stronger.

Have Your Own Life

When you're in a relationship, your partner is usually the first person you turn to for anything. This is a normal thing for us to do but one person can't meet all of your needs. That's why we need friends, family, and our own interests.

Think of your friend group, you probably don't speak about the same thing to every single one of them. One of them is for when you need relationship advice, one of them is for when you would like to talk about books or movies, and one is your person when you need advice about managing your money better. Each of your friends plays a different role in your life and your partner should be the same. It's unfair of you to expect your partner to be your everything. That's also a lot of pressure to put on your partner. You could make them feel as though being with you is a chore and you definitely don't want that.

My partner is the first person I will go to when something exciting happens or if I need to vent, but some things they're just not equipped to deal with such as with the best advice for a particular situation.

Having your own life doesn't stop with your social life though. You need to have hobbies that don't include your partner. Feeling like you have something that's just yours will make you feel more at ease because you won't have the fear that if you and your partner broke up, you will have nothing.

Spend Some Time Alone

When intimacy collapses into fusion, it is not a lack of closeness but too much closeness that impedes desire. Our need for togetherness exists alongside our need for separateness. Thus, separateness is a precondition for connection: this is the essential paradox of intimacy and sex. —Esther Perel, MA, LMFT

When you're in love, you want to spend every waking moment with your partner, but that isn't healthy. It sounds strange to say that you should stay away from your partner for a while in order to improve your relationship, but you need time alone in order for you to improve yourself.

If you're in each other's space all the time, you're going to start getting agitated by many of their habits that seemed small at first. Your partner's nail biting habit that started out as endearing could turn into the bane of your existence if you're hanging around them every day.

It's also extremely isolating to spend all of your time with your partner. I've lost many friends because once they got into a relationship, it was like they ceased to exist. This ties back into having your own life outside of your relationship. A lot of your friends won't be very forgiving if you break up with your partner and you're finally ready to hang out with them again. If this happens, you can experience more anxiety in your relationship because without your partner, you'll have no one.

If you and your partner live together, it's even more important to find a space where you can be alone. Even if you go for a walk for half an hour every day, you'll still have some time that's exclusively for you.

Make Things Exciting

When you're in a long term relationship and you start becoming more comfortable with your partner, it's easy to slip into a routine. I fell victim to this too. My partner and I went from going to new restaurants, going on hikes, and taking weekend trips away to staying in every weekend, ordering take out, and binge watching Netflix. Luckily, I picked up on the routine change and I decided to work on changing things up a bit. I'm a homebody at heart which is why I fell into this comfortable cycle so quickly. Thankfully, we now have a balance of doing fun things and doing nothing at all.

When you switch things up, it keeps your relationship exciting and fun. You don't have to go out to make things exciting. Not everyone enjoys or has the means to try new things all the time. You can still surprise your partner every now and then. You can refer back to their love language to figure out what's the best way to surprise them. Buy them a new gift, visit them when they're not expecting you, offer to clean their home, or randomly write them a cute letter or text to remind them of how much you love them.

Accept That Your Relationship Isn't Perfect

Every relationship has rough patches occasionally despite what other people might make it look like on social media or when they're around other people. You shouldn't punish yourself or your partner when things aren't going smoothly. The sooner you accept that, the sooner you and your partner can start working on improving your relationship instead of dwelling on the negative aspects.

Stay Positive

When things start getting tough, it's difficult to remember any positive memories about your relationship. This is even more true for those with relationship anxiety. So when things are going negatively, thinking back on all the happier times the two of you have had will relieve some of the strain that's on your relationship.

A little trick I found was every time something wonderful happens or your partner does something that makes you smile, write it down and put it in a jar. When you start viewing your relationship negatively, open the jar and take out one of the notes you made. This will help you remember that the relationship isn't all negative.

Conclusion

Every time you are tempted to react in the same old way, ask if you want to be a prisoner of the past or a pioneer of the future. –
Deepak Chopra

Relationships require a lot of hard work, but you should remember that if you hit a rough patch in your relationship, that it's okay. All relationships will have problems at some point and you shouldn't beat yourself up if you have a disagreement with your partner. It's easy to start spiraling when things aren't going as well as you'd like, but if you find yourself falling into anxious patterns, you can come back to this book as a reminder that what you're feeling is normal and you can overcome your anxiety.

If you feel like your relationship anxiety is acting up but you're not completely sure, take a minute to go through the warning signs in chapter one and compare them with your recent behaviors. If it helps, you can even make a check list of the signs. Have you recently started questioning everything your partner is doing? Have you stopped speaking up when something is bothering you? Do you find yourself expecting the worst out of every situation? Have you been asking your partner for reassurance more than usual? Do you think about breaking up with your partner because you think they want to leave you? Are you actively doing things to cause the relationship to end? If you said yes to any of those questions, you should be sure to set aside some time to speak to your partner about your feelings and to do some anxiety reducing exercises. Relationship anxiety won't go away overnight, but it will get easier every day if you stick to the practices in this book.

When your relationship anxiety is high, talking to your partner about your feelings can seem impossible and if you're not ready to take that step yet, that's perfectly fine. You should find an outlet for your feelings though. Talking to your friends, family, or a therapist will help you make better sense of your feelings, but you can even write your feelings out in a journal if you're not up to speaking to anyone. Journaling is a great and healthy outlet for negative feelings. Leaving your thoughts to float around your head will do nothing but increase your anxiety. When you put your thoughts on paper or you speak about them to a loved one, it makes it easier to think of ways to solve the problem.

You have to love yourself to feel fully secure in your relationship. When you have high self-esteem, you're less likely to develop relationship anxiety. Try looking in the mirror every day and say three things you like about yourself. By doing this, you're conditioning your mind to think of yourself in a positive light. When you hear something enough times, you'll start to believe it.

We all feel insecure in our relationships from time to time so remember that even if your partner doesn't have relationship anxiety, you should still be kind and show them you love them. When you make your partner feel happy, you will feel happy too. Take the time to figure out what their love language is so that you can shower them with love in a way that will resonate with them the best. Spend as much time as you can with them and fill up that time with fun activities you two can do together.

Having anxiety in your relationship can be scary, but it doesn't mean the end of your relationship. As you can tell from this book, there are tons of ways you can better your relationship and decrease your anxiety. So go and tell your partner you love them and start working on staying mentally and physically healthy. Take deep breaths, drink tea, practise mindfulness, and love yourself first. Soon, your relationship will go back to being a source of peace and joy instead of anxiety and fear.

References

Ainsworth, M.D.S. & Bowlby, J. (1991). An Ethological Approach to Personality Development. *American Psychologist. 46* (4), 333-341

American Psychological Association. (2021). *Beyond worry: How psychologists help with anxiety disorders.* Apa.org. https://www.apa.org/topics/anxiety/disorders

Ankrom, S. (2021 March 20). *How to breathe properly for relieving your anxiety.* Verywell Mind. https://www.verywellmind.com/abdominal-breathing-2584115

Anxiety and Depression Association of America (ADAA). (2019). *Tips | Anxiety and Depression Association of America, ADAA.* Adaa.org. https://adaa.org/tips

Artful Tea. (n.d.). Calming Tea: The 5 Best Teas for Anxiety and Stress. ArtfulTea. https://www.artfultea.com/tea-wisdom-1/2019/5/1/teas-for-stress-relief

Bhasin, M. K., Denninger, J. W., Huffman, J. C., Joseph, M. G., Niles, H., Chad-Friedman, E., Goldman, R., Buczynski-Kelley, B., Mahoney, B. A., Fricchione, G. L., Dusek, J. A., Benson, H., Zusman, R. M., & Libermann, T. A. (2018). Specific Transcriptome Changes Associated with Blood Pressure Reduction in Hypertensive

Patients After Relaxation Response Training. *Journal of alternative and complementary medicine (New York, N.Y.), 24*(5), 486–504. https://doi.org/10.1089/acm.2017.0053

Bustle. (n.d.). *15 Common Causes Of Anxiety In Relationships.* Bustle. https://www.bustle.com/articles/184035-15-common-causes-of-anxiety-in-relationships

Chapman, G. (1992). *The Five Love Languages: How to Express Heartfelt Commitment to Your Mate.* Moody Publishing.

Gaiam. (n.d.). *8 Ways to Strengthen Your Relationship.* Gaiam. https://www.gaiam.com/blogs/discover/8-ways-to-strengthen-your-relationship

Headspace. (2018). *How to Reduce Anxiety - Headspace.* Headspace. https://www.headspace.com/articles/how-to-reduce-anxiety

Headspace. (2019). *Guided Meditation - Headspace.* Headspace. https://www.headspace.com/meditation/guided-meditation

Healthline. (2019 November 25). *How to Stop Being Codependent in Relationships.* Healthline. https://www.healthline.com/health/how-to-stop-being-codependent#understand-it

Healthline. (2019 November 14). *Relationship Anxiety: 16 Signs and Tips.* Healthline. https://www.healthline.com/health/relationship-anxiety#signs

Healthline. (2020 September 17). *Which Type of Meditation Is Right for You?* Healthline. https://www.healthline.com/health/mental-health/types-of-meditation#getting-started

Hellorelish.com, (n.d.). *What's Your Attachment Style? Anxious, Disorganized, Avoidant or Secure?* Hellorelish.com. https://hellorelish.com/articles/whats-your-relationship-attachment-style.html

Hellorelish.com. (n.d.). *20 Signs You're Experiencing Relationship Anxiety (And How to Cope) - Relish.* Hellorelish.com. https://hellorelish.com/articles/relationship-anxiety-signs.html

Mayo Clinic. (2020). *Can mindfulness exercises help me?* Mayo Clinic. https://www.mayoclinic.org/healthy-lifestyle/consumer-health/in-depth/mindfulness-exercises/art-20046356#:~:text=Mindfulness%20is%20a%20type%20of

McLean, K. (2020, June 12). *Understanding Codependency (Anxious Attachment).* Psychotherapy. https://www.kennedymclean.com/post/understanding-codependency-anxious-attachment#:~:text=Anxious%20attachment%20is%20what%20is

Nguyen, J. (2020 May 19). *Why Everyone's Talking About Love Languages These Days & How To Find Yours.* Mindbodygreen. https://www.mindbodygreen.com/articles/the-5-love-languages-explained

NPR.org. (n.d). *How To Help Your Anxious Partner — And Yourself.* NPR.org. https://www.npr.org/sections/health-shots/2019/07/24/744465884/how-to-help-your-anxious-partner-and-yourself

PsychAlive. (2016 March 4). *How to Deal with Jealousy: Overcoming Overwhelming Jealous Feelings.* PsychAlive. https://www.psychalive.org/how-to-deal-with-jealousy/

Reachout. (2019). *10 tips for improving your self-esteem.* Reachout.com. https://au.reachout.com/articles/10-tips-for-improving-your-self-esteem

Road to Growth Counseling. (2019 July 14). *Ten Ways to Strengthen Your Relationship.* Road to Growth Counseling. https://www.roadtogrowthcounseling.com/ten-ways-to-strengthen-your-relationship/

Rosenberg, M. (2015). Nonviolent Communication: A Language of Life, 3rd Edition: Life-Changing Tools for Healthy Relationships. PuddleDancer Press; Third Edition.

The Centre for Addiction and Mental Health (CAMH). (n.d.). *Anti-Anxiety Medications (Benzodiazepines).* CAMH. https://www.camh.ca/en/health-info/mental-illness-and-addiction-index/anti-anxiety-medications-benzodiazepines#:~:text=Overview-

The Everygirl. (2017 November 17). 10 Things You Can Do to Improve Your Relationship. *The Everygirl.* https://theeverygirl.com/10-things-you-can-do-to-improve-your-relationship/

Verywell Mind. (n.d.). *Why Letting Go of Control Can Help You Enjoy Life*. Verywell Mind. https://www.verywellmind.com/letting-go-of-control-can-help-you-enjoy-life-5208817

Verywell Mind. (n.d.). *How to Distract Yourself From Panic Disorder*. Verywell Mind. https://www.verywellmind.com/distraction-techniques-for-panic-disorder-2584138#:~:text=Instead%20of%20putting%20all%20your

Printed in Great Britain
by Amazon